SELF-MADE MAN

Kevin Thompson

Kevin Thompson

To my mom, who helped fund this book and believed in me. I wouldn't have this without you. Thank you, I love you.

Table of Contents

GLOSSARY

Atheist-a person who disbelieves or lacks belief in the existence of God or gods.

Agender-a term which can be literally translated as 'without gender'. It can be seen either as a non-binary gender identity or as a statement of not having a gender identity.

Androgynous-identifying and/or presenting as neither distinguishably masculine nor feminine.

Anxiety-intense, excessive, and persistent worry and fear about everyday situations.

Asexual-without sexual feelings or associations.

Bigender-someone whose gender identity encompasses both man and woman. Some may feel that one side or the other is stronger, but both sides are present.

Binary-the gender binary is a system of viewing gender as consisting solely of two identities and sexes, man and woman or male and female.

Binder-chest compression vest, tape, etc. used to flatten chest.

Binding-refers to flattening breast tissue to create a male-appearing chest using a variety of materials and methods. binding is a way for many trans men to prevent dysphoria but not all trans men choose to bind.

Biphobia- aversion toward bisexuality and toward bisexual people as a social group or as individuals. It can take the form of denial that bisexuality is a genuine sexual orientation, or of negative stereotypes about people who are bisexual (such as the beliefs that they are promiscuous or dishonest).

Birth (Legal) Name-the name someone has when he or she is born, or at least from the time he or she is a child.

Bisexual-sexually attracted not exclusively to people of one gender; attracted to both men and women.

Bottom Dysphoria-term used to describe one's discomfort with their genitalia mismatching their gender identity.

Bottom Surgery-transform the female genitalia and reconstruct it into that of the opposite sex.

Cisgender-denoting or relating to a person whose sense of personal identity and gender corresponds with their birth sex.

Cisnormativity- the assumption that a person's gender identity matches their biological sex.

Depression-a mental health disorder characterized by persistently depressed mood or loss of interest in activities, causing significant impairment in daily life.

Double Mastectomy-procedure consisting of subcutaneous breast removal.

Estradiol-a major estrogen produced in the ovaries.

Estrogen-any of a group of steroid hormones which promote the development and maintenance of female characteristics of the body.

FTM-Female to Male transgender.

Gay- a man who is attracted to other men; also, sometimes used as an umbrella term for the lesbian, gay, and bisexual community (e.g., the gay community).

Gender Dysphoria-the distress a person feels due to their birth-assigned sex and gender not matching their gender identity. People who experience gender dysphoria are typically transgender.

Gender Identity-the personal sense of one's own gender; can correlate with assigned sex at birth or can differ from it.

Gender Neutral-suitable for, applicable to, or common to all genders.

Genderqueer- denoting or relating to a person who does not subscribe to conventional gender distinctions but identifies with neither, both, or a combination of male and female genders.

Gender Reassignment Surgery (GRS)- also referred to as Gender Confirmation Surgery (GCS) or Sex Reassignment Surgery (SRS), this is a surgical procedure that changes a person's genitalia to match that of their sexual identity.

Heteronormativity- the belief that heterosexuality, predicated on the gender binary, is the norm or default sexual orientation.

Heterosexual- sexually attracted to people of the opposite sex.

Homophobia- encompasses a range of negative attitudes and feelings toward homosexuality or people who are identified or perceived as being lesbian, gay, or bisexual.

Homosexual-sexually attracted to people of one's own sex.

Hormones-special chemical messengers in the body that are created in the endocrine glands. These messengers control most major bodily functions, from simple basic needs like hunger to complex systems like reproduction, and even the emotions and mood.

Hormone Replacement Therapy (HRT)-sex hormones and other hormonal medications are administered to transgender or gender nonconforming individuals for the purpose of more closely aligning their secondary sexual characteristics with their gender identity.

Hysterectomy-operation to remove female reproductive organs.

Ignorance -lack of knowledge or information. Can lead to bullying and/or misinterpretation of a certain subject/topic/aspect/characteristic/action/behavior/thought.

Intersex- individuals born with any of several variations in sex characteristics including chromosomes, gonads, sex hormones, or genitals that, according to the UN Office of the High Commissioner for Human Rights, "do not fit the typical definitions for male or female bodies".

Lesbian- a homosexual woman.

LGBTQIA- an umbrella term that is often used to refer to the entire community: **L**esbian, **G**ay, **B**isexual, **T**ransgender, **Q**ueer, **I**ntersex, **A**sexual, etc.

Metoidioplasty-a term used to describe surgical procedures that work with your existing genital tissue to form what is called a neophallus, or new penis.

MTF-Male to Female transgender.

Pansexual- the sexual, romantic, or emotional attraction towards people regardless of their sex or gender identity.

Passing-or blending refers to someone, especially a transgender person or crossdresser, who is perceived as the gender they wish to be seen as. (For example, a trans woman who is correctly gendered by a store employee who calls her "ma'am").

Phalloplasty-the construction or reconstruction of a penis, or the artificial modification of the penis by surgery.

Queer- an umbrella term for sexual and gender minorities who are not heterosexual or are not cisgender.

Sex Assignment- the determination of an infant's sex at birth based merely on genitalia.

Sexuality-a person's sexual orientation or preference.

Social Anxiety-the fear of being judged and evaluated negatively by other people, leading to feelings of inadequacy, inferiority, self-consciousness, embarrassment, humiliation, and depression.

Stealth-used to refer to a person who always passes as their desired gender.

Suicide-the act of intentionally causing one's own death.

Testosterone-sometimes called "T," it is the main hormone responsible for promoting "male" physical traits and is usually used for hormonal "masculinization" in FTMs. Testosterone works directly on tissues in your body (e.g., stimulating clitoral growth) and indirectly by suppressing estrogen production.

Top (Chest) Dysphoria- term most often used to describe someone's discomfort with their chest and upper body, such as transmasculine people feeling top dysphoria because of their breasts being too big/their shoulders being too slender, or transfeminine people feeling top dysphoria at their lack of breasts/masculine shoulders and arms.

Top Surgery-gender affirming procedure for transgender men and non-binary individuals that creates a masculine chest.

Transgender-denoting or relating to a person whose sense of personal identity and gender does not correspond with their birth sex. Also can be used as an umbrella term, describing anyone who doesn't identify from their assigned sex at birth.

Transition- the process of changing one's gender presentation and/or sex characteristics to accord with one's internal sense of gender identity – the idea of what it means to be a man or a woman, or to be non-binary or genderqueer. (Non-binary people's internal sense of gender identity is neither solely female nor male.) For transgender people, this process commonly involves reassignment therapy (which may include hormone replacement therapy and sex reassignment surgery), with their gender identity being opposite that of their birth-assigned sex and gender. Transitioning might involve medical treatment, but it does not always involve it. Cross-dressers, drag queens, and drag kings tend not to transition, since their variant gender presentations are (usually) only adopted temporarily.

Transman-a man who was assigned female at birth.

Transphobia- the range of negative attitudes, feelings, or actions toward transgender or transsexual people, or toward transsexuality. Transphobia can be emotional disgust, fear, violence, anger, or discomfort felt or expressed towards people who do not conform to society's gender expectations.

Transwoman- a woman who was assigned male at birth.

CHAPTER ONE

The Gift of Life

I never thought I would be able to look like a man. From birth, I had been told how to dress, talk, walk, and act based on the way my body looked. It had always felt wrong and off to act as a female; it wasn't natural for me. The beginning of my life was a performance —I pretended to be a girl, but my mind had always been a boy.

It started on a cloudy, windy Sunday morning. The swishing of scrubs against the floor made the air feel cold. My family was there—grandparents, my mom, my dad. Everyone came to witness a new life coming into the world. I slipped out at about 10:36am, crying because I had been born the wrong sex. My family, distracted by the joy of the atmosphere, never even questioned if their baby girl would eventually become a man. I mean, I don't blame them. Why would they?

We left the hospital after just two days. My mom made a speedy recovery after her natural birth and had already made the decision that she would pursue her usual everyday activities in the upcoming week. She was a pretty hard worker, and she wasn't about to let giving birth slow her down.

My mom was the eldest of three girls. She stayed in my grandparents' house when I was born for help while she was working and going to school. My mom didn't do well in high school, but she knew how to get by. She was able to save money and get her Associate's Degree in education by sacrificing her social life and budgeting fastidiously. She became a substitute teacher the year I was born.

In 2002, my mom got her Bachelor's in Education and began teaching English in elementary schools. My path through childhood was smoothed in many ways as a result of having a parent who was aware of the importance of education. She understood how vital it was for me to start off with access to teachers and a school environment who would nurture my love for learning.

I was born in October and my late birthday meant that I was always one of the youngest kids in my class. That never bothered me, though, and it wasn't long before I had other things on my mind besides being younger than some of the other kids in my class.

Preschool is where my memory of life began, and even in those early days I have a clear recollection of my admiration for women. This is where I caught the first glimpse of my own sexuality. I don't recall much from those days, but I do remember the girl I liked. She was cute and light-skinned with natural curls. I knew that I felt differently towards her than I did the other students, I just didn't know why.

I figured out later in life that this feeling was attraction. From getting nervous to sitting beside her on the bus to chasing her around during recess out of mere admiration, I adored that girl. I wasn't sure if we had been assigned seats on the bus or if we were free to sit wherever, but I knew I spent a lot of time with her. The way the sun shone in the windows of the bus made her brown eyes turn hazel. Her hair was always moist with product, and the familiarity of her Shea butter smell made me feel at home.

I had been born with more hair than the average black girl, and even as a small child I was well acquainted with all the tricks of the hair management trade. For me, hair was always a symbolism of femininity that I wanted to avoid. I dreaded the long and tedious process of painful hairstyles like the hot sizzling of oil on my ear when the hot comb got too close or the headaches from cornrows that stayed tight on my scalp for days at a time. Throughout my life, I would alter my hair to match how I felt inside.

For black women, hair is a very essential piece of their presentation. Our westernized culture in the United States makes black women and men feel insecure about their natural hair textures due to European beauty standards being held up as the basis of "normality."

In preschool, I noticed another change in how I felt about myself; I didn't have the words for it then, but what I was really exploring was my gender identity.

Figuring out who you are and how to successfully navigate the messiness of life is a struggle for everyone, but I started off with an added challenge: I was born into the world as a gender that didn't match who I truly was. Even though society had told me from birth that I was a girl, I never felt that it was accurate. I always gravitated towards masculinity and displaying characteristics that most people expect from men, and not women.

For as far back as I can remember, I never liked anything associated with femininity. If anything, it made me cringe. Being told that I should want to play with dolls and wear frilly pink dresses never sat right with me, but it went deeper than that.

As a five-year-old, I struggled to cope with the constant feeling of wrongness, and I felt like I was stuck in a void of confusion. The concept of not identifying with the sex you were assigned at birth is a complex notion for cis people to understand—and even sometimes for myself.

There were many times growing up where I wanted to shop in the boy's section, but I couldn't because of the bottomless representations of cisnormativity. I longed for the childhood that I saw the boys around me having, and there was always a piece of me that longed to go a step farther and be a boy.

In spite of what I wanted, I knew that being born a girl meant I had to act like one… but why? I silently wondered who created these rules and what the reasons behind them were, but that certainly wasn't a question I could ask out loud.

As you can imagine, all of these dynamics caused me to question and doubt myself. Confidence is one of the most valuable traits to possess as a transgender person. Journeying through decisions that may lead to permanent physical change requires deep internal thought and reflection about what will be gained or lost. Transitioning to live authentically is a very courageous process to undergo. Defying the gender binary is unacceptable and goes against everything society teaches is 'normal' or 'right.' To be able to transition, you need to have a lot of confidence to help bring the person you know you are into existence while knowing that the person you were born as will one day cease to exist. The history of your experience, though, is forever.

As a minority, you notice privilege. Being black and transgender subjected me to two types of oppression that I never asked for. Don't get me wrong, I'm proud of both identities but growing up this way made it harder for me to love myself. Facing these two predetermined and uncontrollable aspects of who I am made me feel that I was not good enough or worthy of love. It would take years before I would become able to accept and appreciate the life I had been given.

CHAPTER TWO

Be My Valentine

As a teacher, my mom knew that different neighborhoods would offer different levels of education quality. So, as soon as preschool days were over, we would be moving to the suburbs of Cheektowaga, a fairly racial diverse town in Buffalo. Our new house was on the border of the city and the suburbs so we wouldn't be too far from the rest of our family, and this is where I first saw the clear divide between the predominantly black city and white suburbia of Buffalo.

Going to a majority white and suburban school doesn't automatically make you smart, though. I had great help shaping my abilities to learn in the academic environments I had access to. The quality of the teachers and resources available at the schools I went to gave me a better chance at success than I would have had if my mom hadn't made education a priority. Having that suburban background early on significantly shaped my character as well.

Past research has exposed the reality behind the sectioning off of certain minority neighborhoods from various kinds of opportunities. Typically, urban areas filled with minorities are separated from schools with quality funding, which in turn limits our youth in some of these most fundamental time periods of growth.

Financial limitations in black neighborhoods also hinder development for businesses that are associated with job opportunities. We don't have access to the variety of stores and resources that suburbs have, and the lack of financial gain keeps our people reliant on government resources. Young people turn to the streets for a way to pay bills, with dreams to one day escape the ghetto.

With poor conditions and no viable options for building a better life, black people suffer from a low quality of life and sometimes turn to drugs to escape the unfairness of this reality.

Drugs that were historically forced into our communities became a way to incarcerate black men into for-profit prisons, reaffirming institutional slavery. The influx of drugs into our communities created a mindset of poverty for those stuck within the barriers of inadequate circumstances.

Drugs continue to be an abundant source of income in black neighborhoods. Locked behind the bars of injustice, our children suffer, falling into the same habits as their mentors in a world where the presence of proper role models is scarce. It's all a cycle of intergenerational oppression.

I was lucky enough to grow up in a stable environment. The only thing that wasn't stable in our household was me. I knew from early on that my sexuality was more fluid than the rigid boundaries that heterosexuality allowed. Even though I had an obvious preference for girls, cute boys would also catch my attention, it just wasn't in a romantic way.

I wasn't yet able to process feelings associated with sex. It's actually pretty normal to admire beauty in the same sex without necessarily being sexually attracted to them. Society imposes strict rules that govern this appreciation of beauty and conflate it with attraction, especially for men. Because of the historical approach to queerness being a negative thing, having your sexuality questioned was dangerous. As a result of this, the process I went through of experiencing both appreciation and the beginnings of attraction is often seen as taboo by broader society.

First grade was my first memory of deviating from the normality of heterosexual standards. It was a cold mid-February day, and knowing Buffalo, the weather was absolute shit. It was the day before Valentine's Day, and my teacher handed out an activity for the holiday.

We had to pick another student in class to be our Valentine so we could get them something and bring it to school. I immediately thought about writing my teacher's name down; her friendly ways with the other children and inviting eyes were captivating. But I ended up choosing one of my fellow female peers.

My teacher walked up to me and looked down at my paper. At the time, I was naive to the societal norms surrounding heterosexuality, so I didn't catch her initial expression, but she was probably one of the first people to know that I liked girls.

She told me I had to pick a boy in the class, not a girl. I remembered being utterly disappointed, probably letting out a muffled "ugh" under my breath as I chose the best male option that I had. This ruined the entire holiday for me and took the excitement from the deepest part of my heart.

It was then that I learned to confine and alter my sexuality due to the primarily negative feedback of my environment. What I experienced in that moment is pretty common for lots of kids who aren't straight, and it made a lasting impression on me. Those who dare to question their sexuality are made out to be inferior by society, and if you don't adhere to societal expectations, you can end up being targeted with verbal, emotional, and physical attacks.

Many kids in the LGBTQ+ community also struggle when it comes to allowing themselves to be authentic. The lack of positive examples and representation from each community creates a stereotype without inclusion of individuals like myself. Everyone suffers from bullying, and while kids are still young, jokes concerning gender and sexuality hit harder considering how intimate and sensitive these aspects of life can be.

42% of all transgender people attempt suicide at least once in their life. Rates of domestic violence and depression are also significantly higher for trans people. No wonder—life sucks sometimes as a trans person. Not only do you not like yourself, but you face pressures from a society that does not approve of who you are.

In spite of some of the positive aspects of my early years, most of it feels like a surreal nightmare, or like something that happened to someone else. I couldn't play with the toys I wanted to or play sports I wanted or generally be seen or treated like the boy I knew I was. As I moved through first grade, family members and friends started to catch on to my ways as a "tomboy."

I clung to this term with no shame because it had boy literally in the name. Looking back, it's hard to connect to the person I was before I knew who I was inside.

CHAPTER THREE

Family Part One

One of my mom's closest friends, Katherine, told her she thought I was gay in the midst of these early years. Many parents feel ashamed when their children come out of the closet, which is why pride is frequently so celebrated in LGBTQ+ culture.

My mom, as well as many other people who knew me, initially considered my identity to be a stigma, so she lashed out at her friend. Being gay, trans, or bisexual doesn't degrade your character. Judging others based on traits we are born with degrades character and shows insecurity, ignorance, and lack of confidence within yourself.

Having a child is very unpredictable. It comes with great amounts of responsibility and selflessness —not to mention all the money that you'll never see again, unless your kid becomes a millionaire and decides to share. Other than that, you basically get screwed financially.

For both of my parents, having a child helped them develop a sense of responsibility. I was her first child, and my mom quickly began to realize how much work goes into parenting. Luckily, she had the help of my dad's family too.

My grandma, or nana as I call her, and aunt would keep me a lot during the beginning stages of my youth to relieve my mom of parenting duties. Nana had been in and out of retirement since I was born but worked for the IRS for the majority of my life. Auntie started working at the Verizon in downtown Buffalo after being discharged from the military. Both these women spent their entire lives on the phone.

My mom had more help on her side. My granny, my grandpa, and two other sisters who were both younger than her. We all lived together at the start but I grew up never calling either of them aunt. By the time I was born, my mom's sister Mariah, who was the second oldest of the three, had a daughter, Kayla, who was already 10 months old.

Kayla and I played together a lot, but we would always get into little fights about toys and I would end up in tears —but it was never the girl toys that I cried over. I reflect on these times and, as a child who literally went through an identity crisis, I would say that I suffered from depression without ever realizing it.

My internal discomfort came out in different ways, like when I would get irritable over the tiniest of things or be devastated about relatively minor hiccups; it was always there. Megan, who was the youngest of the three sisters, had a daughter named Iyana when I was two. Megan was the only one out of the three to stay in the childhood home for years following her daughters' birth.

Having a child at the age of twenty-two can put limits on how you move through life. You're constrained and essentially stuck with the responsibility of being a parent. My dad had an easier time with this since my mom won custody of me.

The fact that society still holds fast to gender roles astounds me. In this era, women have become more independent and involved in the workplace but are still held accountable for household burdens and raising kids. They are expected to do men's jobs and more, all while being paid less and treated as inferiors. Sexism lies in gender roles.

I was one of my dad's two kids. My little brother and I were half-siblings and shared the same father. My brother's mom also won custody of him and decided to move to Indiana while he was still young. He's the type of kid who needed some extra support to be successful, but his parents' pride got in the way so he suffered through life and school.

My brother didn't visit Charlotte as frequently as I did. Spending those summers in the south with my dad created a "bond" between us that never existed between him and my brother. My dad yearned for that father-son relationship, but he refused to have that with me in later years even when he had the chance.

My dad and I started off "cool." Back when he lived in Buffalo, he'd watch me every once in a while. He had always been into money and I guess I subconsciously noticed this as a child. He would always buy different kinds of candy in bulk sizes for redistribution amongst coworkers. He did the same thing before I was born, but it wasn't candy he was selling. He sold sweet words and lies to the people he knew while they would never know the bitterness beyond the wrapper.

CHAPTER FOUR

Family Part Two

In the beginning it was just me and my mom living in some apartments off Section 8. My mom moved out of her parents' house when I was still in preschool. We started off using social services to get by.

The work ethic my mom had was passed down from my granny. There were many steps my mom took in her early years that became essential to her success as an adult. Choosing to go back to school allowed her to move out and get her name on a mortgage at 25 years old.

Years later, she would tell me that this motivation came from the duties and responsibilities she knew came with parenthood. When my mom grew up, she was treated more harshly than her sisters. Maybe it was because she was the oldest, but I don't think it was a coincidence that she became arguably the most successful of the three sisters.

My mom took me to church frequently as a child, probably because she grew up in the church as well. In the US, people are often shunned for not believing in God, but it was never a belief system I could understand. We want to know that this isn't "it," that we will be able to see our loved ones again after death while our spirits are able to roam free at heaven's gate.

Sounds good, but almost too good to be true. There's been no evidence of anything in the afterlife, so how can so many people be so sure in following these notions?

There were many things I couldn't understand growing up. One of life's many aspects that I held no answers to was the reason behind why my parents weren't together. They had split before I was born, so I had never even seen how they were with each other. In school I would hear my classmates talk about their home life, and it always included two heterosexual parents.

Not only is sexuality amongst parents stereotyped, but the assumption is that there must be two. Some parents single-handedly take care of children who, if adequately kept, don't suffer from the loss of the other parent's presence.

Even with steady strides toward proper representation, television continues to show mostly female/male relationships. Most children are not exposed to different kinds of family dynamics, let alone any type of queer relationship. Exposure to the LGBTQ + community is important for development in young children so they don't grow up stereotyping certain identities and preferences; this kind of ignorance leads to bullying when children can't relate to queer struggles.

For kids who don't yet know they are a part of the community, it's difficult to develop a healthy sense of identity without terms and role models that are able to define their experiences. This lack of awareness within human nature creates depression, confusion, and insecurities, which makes growing up that much harder. I wish I had known more about the realm of gender and sexual spectrums as a child; it would've made my hell a bit more bearable.

My dad had no real other relationships that I knew of growing up. He was a player, and these days, I don't blame him. It's a lot easier to move around from woman to woman than to invest time, money, and emotional attention into a person who might eventually end up hurting the deepest parts of you. What a stupid risk, right? But the things people do for love, I guess. My dad didn't do a lot to get attention from women, but he used me as part of his "game" once I was old enough to speak.

One summer in Charlotte, back when we still ate meat, my dad took me to a place in the south called Steak and Shake. He told me to follow this lady in the women's bathroom and had a specific line in mind for me to repeat once I had gathered her attention.

He did this often, even in Buffalo, and sometimes, the shit worked. Kids are highly unattractive in my opinion, but that's also coming from a man who doesn't like kids. These women probably thought it was cute. I walked in awkwardly and tried to imagine being in the woman's shoes, having a guy hit on me with his kid. Yeah, no thanks.

I was a pretty well-mannered child and knew how to converse, smile, and be polite whenever I was in public. Spending the majority of my life depressed meant that I learned how to fake a pretty believable smile. I kept up the attitude of always smiling even if I wasn't happy. It scared me to have people question negative signs in my mood because most of the time it was related to my identity—something I still hate talking about with most people. It would be hard for me to tell others what I was feeling when I still didn't have answers as to why I felt the way I did. I also started learning how to smile if I ever felt uncomfortable or nervous. Putting a smile on as a mask quickly taught me that the phrase "fake it till you make it" had a lot of truth behind it.

My mom was more into dating than messing around. She had a few relationships that I vaguely remember. The best part is that they were all really nice to me—until her third boyfriend, Walter.

Walter was a different kind of guy for my mom. All of her previous boyfriends had been what you might call bums. Walter was a pretty nerdy and corny guy that went to college, got some degrees, and became a principal.

After my mom got her bachelor's degree and got her own classroom, they ended up working at the same school. After meeting, they bonded over the importance of education within inner city school districts. His obvious educational and career success made my mom's lower-income side of the family really appreciate her new romantic choice.

At the age of seven, I could tell how important of a person he was. Walter was well-known in Buffalo for his work at multiple different schools in the city. He helped my mom with her own career and educational goals. Their relationship seemed like an arranged marriage through the Buffalo Public School system. I could see that she really liked him, but I was not convinced on his character.

Unlike the other men in my mom's life, Walter never reached out for a relationship with me. My mom noticed the distance between us but thought we would come to be comfortable with each other over time. My quiet persona had no direct problems with his choice of not getting to know me, but I knew something was off about it.

As an adult, he hadn't filled the duty of taking initiative to establish a bond between the two of us. By the time I had gotten older and had the choice to reach out, it was too late. I didn't care anymore, and neither did he.

He moved in just a few months after they started dating. Before living with my mom and I, Walter lived a bachelor lifestyle in an apartment complex with his brother Mark, who I had a better relationship with. No one ever knew, but Walter really wanted a lifestyle consisting of minimal obligations.

Unfortunately for the people around him, he was quickly sucked into societal norms surrounding mortgages and parental responsibilities after marriage. The conflict between what he wanted and what he ended up with helped explain the reasons behind what Walter did to my mom and I, but that didn't make it hurt any less.

My immediate family grew from two to three people seemingly overnight. Walter's presence completely altered the dynamic of our home since I now had, not only a stranger, but a man living with me.

I had never really lived with any men growing up before Walter. The weekends I spent with my dad before he moved and the summers I lived in Charlotte didn't come close to the amount of time I'd spend living with Walter. Even though we were under the same roof, Walter and I barely communicated. Suppressed awkward tensions at home would follow us out to family functions and in public spaces.

Walter was supposed to be a good figure in my life. He was one of the first male role models from my childhood, but I never wanted to be anything like him. The guy had the most "cringe" characteristics. I didn't hate him yet, but my dislike would begin to boil after each unnecessary or weird interaction.

My mom would often compare our personalities, but if anything, we'd only have emotional levels and intelligence in common. Granted, I had been depressed and anxious my entire life due to LGBT issues, but maybe Walter was still just as insecure as I was at the time. Walter always portrayed an exterior shell that not even his own mother could break through.

Sometimes my mom would tell me about how he cried over stressful situations, and I pondered on how embarrassed he would be to know she'd told me. Unconsciously, I always jumped at an opportunity to make him as uncomfortable as he would make me for several years in that home. I wasn't trying to be cruel, but it gave me satisfaction knowing we were, at the very least, on the same comfort level.

My dad had been uneasy about the new living situation. I assumed my dad wouldn't totally approve of his little girl living with a man he didn't know. Many dads are naturally protective of their children, especially when unfamiliar men are spending a lot of time with them, but my dad never had to worry about Walter saying anything inappropriate to me or trying to discipline me because we barely talked. I never got close enough with Walter to call him dad and never felt the need to. After all, I did have an-other dad in my life out there.

CHAPTER FIVE

Glitter Overdose

My mom and Walter got married the summer after first grade. When they made me the flower girl, I wasn't necessarily opposed to the role. I was seen as a girl and I knew that being part of the wedding in this way was a kind of duty for me, no discussion. My mom got my hair straightened and lightly curled. Not gonna lie, I looked pretty good for the occasion, but I didn't associate the person in the mirror with myself.

That wasn't the first time I dressed up to be the flower girl in a wedding. In some ways it was nice to be complimented by strangers on my appearance, but the actual compliments were designated for the wrong sex. I wanted to be handsome, not beautiful, and certainly not with long hair in a dress. I was just glad I wasn't old enough for heels and make up.

I was a compliant kid growing up. I always listened and wasn't the type to talk back. Who am I kidding, I barely talked at all because of all the suppressed emotions. I didn't know how to express myself without feeling out of place. So I did what was told; it's easier to follow than to lead.

My mom and aunt Mariah put me and my cousin Kayla in cheerleading that summer. Even though I'd rather have played football with the guys, I was pretty good at cheering. My coach assigned me as one of two co-captains my very first year. I don't remember being particularly advanced within the group, but I guess my coach thought otherwise.

The next summer I came back to the team a few weeks late since I had been staying with my dad. When I returned, the coach informed me I would be the captain during the upcoming season. The fact that I still received this position even after missing the first couple weeks of practice confounded me.

I was shocked that the coaches saw so much potential in me, but the overwhelming positive feedback and attention had a negative side. I wanted nothing to do with this stereotypical female sport, and it made me cringe that everyone saw me as being talented at it.

My family loved coming to the games. They knew I was a tomboy and enjoyed seeing me excel at such a feminine activity. They weren't really educated about LGBTQ+ issues, which was why I tried so hard to repress the emotions I felt due to dysphoria and avoided confronting family members about the psychological difficulties that I faced. I knew that they would never be able to relate to my struggles, and I worried about what their response would be.

Once I realized I wasn't comfortable with my assigned gender, I became very quiet and cautious with my mannerisms. This alteration in mental state began around first and second grade due to gender dysphoria and insecurities surrounding my sexual preference for women.

There wasn't a term for me when I was growing up to describe what I later learned was dysphoria. Family gatherings showcased my mental health issues years before I would ever reflect on them in counseling. Insecurities surrounding my gender presentation created problems with social anxiety very early on. It was hard to act enthused about new items or gifts, which made people view me as ungrateful.

For Christmas I would always get presents similar to those of my cousins, Kayla and Iyana. When anyone would ask what I wanted,

I tried to stay as neutral as possible with my choices so as not to give any hint of my true identity.

I was fortunate enough to grow up in the age of modern technology, which allowed me to confide in electronics, but that didn't make holidays or family gatherings any easier. The adults in my life caught on to my ambivalence towards girly items, but they never strayed too far from the glitter when buying gendered things for me.

One year, Kayla and I both got the same gift: a purple Bratz-themed winter coat. When my mom gave it to me, I immediately started crying. As an already depressed and anxious child, I cried because I wasn't able to adequately vocalize my discomfort and I knew I would have to suffer through wearing the jacket in the cold bitter winter.

Before I even put it on, I knew how much humiliation I would feel from having to go out in public in that thing—ew. My family, not knowing how I really felt inside, didn't help the feelings of depression that inevitably arrived because of my situation. When I became more aware of my discomfort with feminine items, I attempted to buy masculine clothes and avoid toys like dolls or anything pink.

When second grade began, I wanted to stay consistent with my passive approach to choices concerning gender, but I also wanted to secretly steer my family away from feminine stereotypes. I started the process in the shopping section.

I had a minor say in clothing choice if I went, so if something looked too out of character, I could tell my mom I disliked it. People caught on to my style and started saying, "Oh yeah, T doesn't like anything girly," because some girls don't. Valid, they just didn't know that wasn't really the case with me.

My case was being embarrassed every time I was called pretty, she, or her. My case was suffering and not being able to develop proper relationships because of mental health struggles. My case was spending my childhood depressed, confused, and hopeless because of things I was born with. I felt hopeless a lot, and I still do even after accomplishing so much surrounding my transition. There's only so much you can do to present as cis when you're not, and I knew that, but I still yearned to get as close as possible.

The day before second grade, I had a conversation with someone that clarified what I ultimately desired in life. I had gotten this outfit for the first day and it had this collar that I thought was super masculine. It was more gender neutral than anything, but to be able to give a first impression without the presence of female attributes made me feel more like myself than I ever had before. I knew from church that people prayed when they wanted something and even though I didn't believe in monotheistic religion, I spoke to God that whole day.

"God, if you could please make me into a boy by tomorrow when I wake up, I'll be so happy and thankful."

"I would never ask for anything ever again."

That is all I've ever wanted. My whole life, all I've wanted is to be a man.

It was a big moment in my childhood for me to reflect on as a transguy. It doesn't get any clearer than that moment. I told myself I wanted to be a boy and brushed it off like some dust on my shoulder. I was in denial about who I was for years after this incident, but thinking back makes me wonder how much time I wasted as a girl.

CHAPTER SIX

English

After my first-grade incident on Valentine's Day, I decided to take advantage of the fact that boys were attracted to me. Since I was presenting as female, I knew that girls who liked me weren't interested in other "girls." I knew they would never give me a shot because of my image. This forced me to turn to guys, because I wanted to feel validated and desirable; the attention put my insecurity at ease.

I knew I was good looking, but I would become very insecure about my inability to never get girls. The hardest part was that I knew they would be attracted to my mind—and to me—if only I looked on the outside how I felt on the inside. Those years were very frustrating for me.

My first kiss was a white boy. His name was Ben and he had the worst breath, but the constant attention from him made me feel like I was complying with societies rules. I sought out his validation and romantic attention. In the future, I would continue to allow boys to pursue me since I thought I'd be rejected in any efforts to pursue girls.

I never had any difficulties with schoolwork throughout my educational career, but second grade was a different situation. That was the year my elementary school began testing for reading and writing skills. They had a testing procedure called DIBLES that analyzed English skills. DIBELS were scored on the student's ability to read an abundance of text in a timely fashion and then answer a post-reading questionnaire that assessed comprehension. Even though my grades were great, I didn't do well on that particular assessment.

I've always been a slow reader, but it didn't mean that I was a slow student. When my teacher discovered that I was reading in a lower percentile compared to other kids, it was decided that I should be placed in a special education class environment for the following school year.

I liked to think of myself as a smart individual, and it was hard to face the fact that the school system had put me in a special education classroom. My mom wasn't a fool to the process since she did the same with her own students. She knew my abilities to read slowly didn't affect my ability to develop significant contextual understandings because some of her students, under the same time restriction, failed to comprehend at all. Even though she could've fought the school to put me in a regular classroom, she let me spend my third-grade year with Mr. Reagan.

I couldn't be more thankful that my mom let me stay in that class with him. The foundation of the skill sets I learned with Mr. Reagan became critical to my future success in reading and writing. English is one of the subjects in school that will always follow you throughout life. I honestly can't say I would be writing this book if it wasn't for my experience with him, so thank you Mr. Reagan.

Third grade was a great time. My entire class was made up of boys and one other girl who eventually moved halfway through the school year. I technically became the only girl in the class at that time, but thinking back, the classroom was really all boys. The abundance of males made me feel like one of them. I was always disappointed when I was reminded that I wasn't a boy, like when it was time to go to the bathroom or when we had to change for gym.

Mr. Reagan had the coolest reward system for getting good grades. There was a literal basketball hoop in our class, and each student would be allotted a certain number of shot attempts depending on which letter grade we received. I had started playing ball at the young age of three, which gave me the ability to hold the highest score in consecutive made attempts. He made learning fun by incorporating my favorite sport; it was an overall quality environment for me.

After my mom and Walter got married, they decided to move to a house deeper in the suburbs. For me, this meant a switch in schools. Our family made the move in December of 2007, halfway through my third-grade year but I would be finishing the school-year with my boys before switching schools.

Toward the end of the academic year, my mom could see how my English skills had improved. To this day, my mom reminds me of how great an influence Mr. Reagan had been for me. It's good to have focused help sometimes, and working with Mr. Reagan got me ready for my fourth grade teacher at my new school.

Mrs. Rachel's fourth grade class was at least a step and a half up from Mr. Reagan's curriculum. From the start, I could tell she was a hard ass. She was tough, but I developed diligence trying to keep up with the work she gave, and in return, obtained a lifelong trait that held the key to success for me. The tools that I learned in Reagan's class were sharpened, and I hit the ground running once fourth grade came along.

That was the year I came to terms with the fact that I wouldn't be able to date girls, but it never stopped me from developing crushes on them. Kate was the second girl that I remembered liking throughout my childhood, and if you remember my type then you know exactly what she looked like. She was a light-skinned Hispanic girl with loose curls and soft eyes.

That was also the first time I distinctly remember not being able to imagine my future, although I knew why. It was because I couldn't see myself marrying a man, and I definitely couldn't see myself birthing a child. The thought of pregnancy and being called mother for the rest of my life sounded like the most feminine act I could ever commit. But I thought that maybe other girls felt like this too, and I thought it was something I would eventually have to get used to.

I never had trouble making friends despite my social anxiety. Normally in elementary grades, students tend to make friends with the same gender because they can relate to each other. I took note of this and did the same to avoid being singled out and questioned about my inner feelings.

I still had friendships with the opposite sex, but I limited the interactions. Another reason for my abundant female friendships was comfortability. My entire family had been comprised of mainly women. That was the gender I had become used to socializing with. Men were foreign to me.

My first "friend" at my new school was Aaliyah. She lived at the end of my street, and I clung to her since there were only a handful of kids my age in the neighborhood. Aaliyah introduced me to her other friends, Gale and Tia. Gale was cool, but Tia and I being of primarily the same race eventually got closer.

She was mixed with mostly black and Asian and unlike anyone I had ever met. We spent all day after school talking and laughing on my house phone. Tia was lowkey my type, but at the time I didn't like her in that way. Her mom scared the crap out of me, so when we hung out, she would always come to my place.

Back in middle school, each school bus had specific destinations, so we needed our parents' permission if we wanted to go to each other's houses. One day Tia came home with me without our parents' permission. I was shocked at her lack of fear and started pondering other kids' relationships with their parents.

Parenting styles vary across culture, location, religion, and so much more. It amazes me how parents have ultimate authority over their children. But it scares me because I know that people —and this world—are cold. Depending on the parent, some kids can get screwed mentally due to cruel upbringings. Have you ever heard that it all starts in the household?

Parents should tailor how they discipline their children to fit specific needs for the child. All kids need adequate discipline and help learning about healthy boundaries and respect. All parents should practice creating open communication between themselves and their children. How can you solve a problem if you don't even know what the problem is?

My mom and I have lots of similarities, including social anxiety and being arguably too friendly to undeserving people, but we also differ in our perspectives on many things. As an optimist, I normally give people the benefit of the doubt. Throughout my life, I have been a really nice person to many undeserving people. I ended up having to cut a lot of people off because they overstayed their welcome in my life and became toxic.

Once Tia and I developed a close and honest relationship, she revealed that Aaliyah had secret motives for being my friend. Aaliyah would make fun of me to our two other friends when I wasn't around. I quickly dropped her as a friend. I had no problems with cutting out toxicity once I felt that a person did something to me that I would never do to them.

I consider myself to be at my best when I'm alone, so I learned how to be alone without feeling lonely; I even preferred it sometimes. Some people go through their whole lives without being able to feel content in physical isolation. The result is chasing meaningless relationships of any kind, even toxic ones, to fill what can only be filled by oneself.

CHAPTER SEVEN

Shifts

I made more friends in fifth grade after joining band. The first year I played percussion, which was affirming since it's historically been seen as a masculine instrument. Yes, this world is so scared of ambiguity and desperate for labels that we gender instruments.

I tried out various other instruments as a kid, but I'd always avoid the feminine ones like flutes and clarinets; those sections were almost always filled with girls. The fear of not wanting to be associated with my biological sex prevented me from enjoying anything even remotely feminine.

There was one childhood friend that I hung onto during this time named Ella. My aunt used to always comment on how much she would text me. Some people might have viewed Ella's actions as annoying, but as a person who sees the glass as half full, I was grateful that the friendship was never one-sided. She had always cared about my other friends and family.

For my tenth birthday that year, I invited Ella, Tia, Gale, and some other girls I had gotten close with in the last year. I had a huge sleepover with around ten girls in my fully furnished basement. It was a pretty equal white to minority ratio. Being a suburban black kid, I always had two sides to me. For a while, I was afraid to be seen as two-faced, but I noticed that I only felt like this when it came to my other black peers. I knew the white people wouldn't care anyway; if anything, they thought I was cool and unique.

Over the years, I've learned to embrace the different aspects of my personality and call it versatility. For me and many others, part of the challenge of growing up comes from developing self-love for all aspects of who you are. But I, like many LGBTQ+ people, dealt with regular insecurities plus the parts of my identity that concern sexuality and gender. The high rates of suicide previously mentioned develop out of frustration with ones' uncontrollable imperfections.

For a few glorious hours at my sleepover, though, I was in heaven. A bunch of fairly attractive girls were all sleeping over my house with me—for me. I felt like the man. My mom, just like any other black mom of course, acted very nice when my friends were around but would go off on me in a second behind closed doors if I acted up. Sometimes I was even shocked at how nice she could be in public.

Nonetheless, I was grateful for her friendly attitude around others. When I would meet my mom's friends, I'd be sure to be on my best behavior as well, partly because I had to. As my mom taught me, we represent each other by our actions and even our looks. All the girls at my house that night kept saying how pretty my mom was. I didn't really notice before and began to look at other people's moms afterward.

I knew I took after my mom in looks when I was called pretty, but every time I looked in the mirror I would cringe inside. Something was clearly off, but since it wasn't an obvious problem, I had done my best to conceal and disregard the feelings. I could never quite connect with the person who looked back at me all of those years, and I only looked in the mirror if I had to. As a person who was very distant from myself, the world became new after transitioning.

When it was time for fifth grade moving-up day, my mom picked out this long black dress with light and dark pink straps. It was girly, but it could've been worse, so I didn't think about it too much. The worst part about having to dress up was always the presentation. My mom always commented on my posture, telling me to walk and sit up straighter. It was so out of the norm of my natural masculine feelings.

These comments were like reminders that I wasn't who I felt like. I didn't want to call myself a boy because I obviously wasn't, but I knew I wasn't really a girl.

Some of the other woman family figures that I had would also passively comment about how I needed to act like a girl. The knowledge they ingrained in me made me feel that it was wrong to be the way I was and that I could eventually learn to become something I wasn't.

Luckily, my mom was the only person to confront me about my masculinity on a regular basis. If Walter had taken more of a fatherly role, he probably would have commented too.

At the end of fifth grade, Walter and I finally found something to bond over: Marvel stuff. When it came to superheroes, Walter was a Marvel geek. He spent his whole life collecting comic books, and when he moved in with us, they appeared all over the house. The living room, their bedroom, even the bathroom for those "number two" moments. Don't even get me started on the dining room —shit was covered, but we never ate there anyway except for when we hosted Thanksgiving. My mom thought it was a waste of space, but there were only so many places he could store them since he had thousands.

Walter took me to get my first set of comic books when I was ten, and that's when I started my collection. It was a Black Widow series of four. We even started playing Marvel games together on my PS2 and on his PS3, and sometimes we would watch tv shows like Everybody Hates Chris as a family with my mom.

These were some of the only times we interacted. The two of them would always tease me about not fully understanding the humor behind the dry jokes on tv, but Walter made fun of me way more. It seemed as though he only had something to say if it consisted of making fun of me in some kind of way.

As an adult-child relationship, it was awkward and very immature on his part, even though our general dislike for each other was definitely mutual. I eventually began returning the jokes in defense after accepting that that's how our relationship would function. I don't enjoy clowning people, but if you come at me, I'll reciprocate the same energy.

One of the first trans people I ever met turned out to be my friend Jake. We weren't super close in school, but I knew deep down that I wanted to present myself the way that he did. When Jake first came to my school in sixth grade, he looked completely male. I remember the first time I saw Jake, he was the new kid who sat alone at lunch. My friends started talking about a girl who looked like a boy and pointed over to him. I didn't believe them at first because of how well he passed.

"They said he went into the girl's locker room to change for gym." Back then, Tia had all the tea.

She told the table his name was Jill to confirm his assigned sex as female. I was still in disbelief.

After a couple of days seeing Jake eat alone, my friends and I decided to go sit with him. We made him feel more comfortable in his new surroundings and I'm glad we did. Being an outcast at such a young age can be hard, especially when few kids understand the complexities that surround aspects of being queer. I was secretly intrigued by his lifestyle. He encompassed everything I didn't know I wanted to be.

At that time, Jake didn't express any feelings of liking women or being trans even though it was evident to the majority. Everyone called him "she" and "Jill" even though neither of the terms fit. He never corrected anyone, so it was what it was.

I recently asked Jake about his experience as a transman who was privileged enough to present as male for basically the entirety of his life. He said he didn't know he was trans until later on and that he was just living the life that he felt right about. It made me realize how each trans person's experience can drastically vary; some people begin their social transition halfway into their lifetime.

For me, the process was more dramatic than Jake's since everyone had watched me attempt to live as a female at the start. Jake had essentially always looked like a guy, so the only social transition he made had been the name and pronouns. When it came time to medically transition, hormones just amplified what he was already putting out. I admired how Jake was able to live authentically all of these years.

The start of middle school was when I began to see the shift in kids heading toward opposite poles on the gender spectrum. It gave me anxiety knowing that I was responsible for fulfilling female duties since all my female friends started maturing physically and doing girly activities together.

Everyone's actions moving toward their gender identity made me feel like the time had come for me to accept my assigned sex and start the battle in my mind with any and all kinds of masculine urges. Little did I know that this shift in others was unconscious; I shouldn't have had to force myself to one side of the gender spectrum when I was really on the other.

My fear of not conforming to expectations about my gender pressured me to prove my womanhood through my sexuality. Since I could tolerate having a boyfriend, I figured I would go that route. I talked to about five guys that year, one being my gay friend Kendrick who would awkwardly kiss me on the cheek between bells.

Some of the guys I was with weren't all that bad, but I didn't want to be with them either, and after Kendrick I knew boys wouldn't work out for me in the long haul. The relationships were always innocent and nothing serious. Kissing, holding hands, and texting once I got my first phone; relationships back then weren't anything like they are now as an adult. I still wonder how those guys who liked me before feel now that I look like them.

Sixth grade brought one of the worst things that could ever happen to a transguy: menstruation. I was prepared for it since my mom gave me a kid's book that explained it in a nice and friendly way.

It was scary, I thought, bleeding excessively for days every month. It already sucked being a girl and then that happened. My mom had given me menstrual cycle info at the perfect time since I got it a few months after I got the book. I gave the book to my cousin Kayla after I got my first period since she hadn't gotten hers yet. It happened at my nana's house.

Thankfully I knew what a period was, or else I probably would've thought I was dying. I don't remember my grandma's comments about the awful occurrence, but my aunt and her boyfriend were there and I loathed their reactions.

"Congratulations, you're a woman now."

Geez, I still remember feeling my face fall after hearing that. Congratulations?! Yes, I'm so happy that I'm a boy now bleeding out of his vagina with yet another reason to be mislabeled as female. It was like involuntarily moving closer to femininity on the spectrum. Amazing news? No, I instantly felt inferior because now I was further from who I wanted to be and further from what I imagined myself as.

At this point, manhood seemed like a distant and impossible dream. The start of my menstrual cycle was another "you're a girl" reminder that I didn't need, like a confirmation that my body's creation as a girl was correct after all.

CHAPTER EIGHT

Double Dribble

Megan—my mom's youngest sister—had a daughter named Maya during my fourth grade year. At that point, Maya was the youngest grandkid. That didn't last long, and we had another baby on the way when Mariah got pregnant with Bennett while I was in fifth grade.

It was the beginning of sixth grade year when my mom and Walter gave me news of their own. I remember how big of a deal it felt like when they called me to the living room to make the announcement. She told me that she was having not only one baby but two. They were twins.

I was excited to see another addition to our family of three. I welcomed the idea even as my anxiety began to worsen. I knew that the twins' presence would take some of the attention off of me. It also seemed like a welcome reprieve from the constant lack of communication in our home. I generally enjoyed the quiet, but it got old after a while.

Once Walter and my mom passed the honeymoon phase of constantly traveling together and expressing the lovey dovey qualities that are so common at the beginning of a relationship, I noticed them shift into a more routine kind of marriage. They didn't look like the couples on tv anymore or even look as happy as they used to. I knew something was different, but it wasn't obviously unhealthy, so it became my idea of marriage years down the road.

Every year our middle school organized a three-day camping trip for the sixth graders. We stayed in cabins, but the experience was still unfamiliar for most of us. It was a fun time in a new surrounding. I had a lot of firsts there; first time hiking, first bonfire, first time canoeing. I even tipped one of my friend's canoes in the water as I was trying to help her steer in the right direction. I felt so bad, but we laughed about it afterward.

Throughout the whole trip I was worried about missing my siblings' birth. With their due date quickly approaching, I knew labor could be induced at any point. When my mom picked me up from the school trip, she looked like she was ready to bust, and I was glad that I hadn't missed their first breath. After we got home, I started making grilled cheese for the two of us—one of the only things I knew how to make at the time—when my mom got a call. The hospital told her to come in to deliver the babies.

Before I had left for the field trip, my stepdad, mom, and I had spent days in the hospital keeping a close eye on the twins because of my mom's declining health during her pregnancy. Many women experience hardships during infant delivery—especially those of African American descent.

Without guaranteed quality healthcare and with tragically common discrimination from healthcare facilities, pregnancies for black women can be difficult and nearly fatal. According to a 2018 report from the National Partnership for Women and Families:

Black women in the United States experience unacceptably poor maternal health outcomes, including disproportionately high rates of death related to pregnancy or childbirth. Both societal and health system factors contribute to high rates of poor health outcomes and maternal mortality for Black women, who are more likely to experience barriers to obtaining quality care and often face racial discrimination throughout their lives. Black women are three to four times more likely to experience a pregnancy-related death than white women.

I hadn't even finished cooking, let alone even started to unpack, and I was suddenly packing an overnight bag for the hospital. My stepdad wasn't home yet, but he would meet us there. We waited for hours for my brother to face head down so my mom could go through with the natural birth, but he wouldn't budge.

My mom ended up having to undergo a C-section instead. The twins were born at four in the morning. All I remember is my granny yelling at me to wake up once the nurses rolled them into the room. I had still been tired from not getting enough sleep on those hard ass cabin beds.

There are approximately 8.3 million different genetic combinations for each human. I immediately started thinking about what kind of people they would be. What they would look like? Would they wear glasses like their parents and me? Would they be nice?

The twins were born June 11th, and with summer quickly approaching I had to make the choice of going to see my dad or staying around with my immediate family and the newborns. At that point, I had been regularly going to see my dad for the summers in Charlotte, but sixth grade was the first time I didn't go since he moved. I had to help my mom out.

I knew two babies would be way more difficult than one. I wasn't mad, though; summers were only ever alright with him. I never even got the bedroom he promised, which was supposed to have a dresser, a proper bed frame, maybe even a little décor. Year after year I was let down by his inability to actually care about the comfortability surrounding my summer living environment. I didn't really have any real friends down there either, so the atmosphere quickly became dull.

The first summer with the twins was really hard for my family, especially my mom. Walter and my mom continued shifting away from each other after the twins' arrival, in part due to the fact that Walter had never been a father before and didn't really know how to handle it. At first, I figured he considered time away from home as a break.

But he didn't consider if my mom needed a break when he spent all that time at work, or when he would randomly and frequently leave the house with every excuse in the book to validate his absence. My granny came to help; she probably felt like it was part of her duty since she helped raise all the grandkids. My mom was grateful to have her mom during this time since she wasn't in a great place mentally and emotionally. She didn't know how to handle two infants simultaneously, and she was also trying to deal with the scar from her C-section incision healing improperly. It was a lot for anyone.

Fortunately for everyone, it got easier, and the whole family returned to school in September while the babies went to my granny's. Walter and my mom didn't feel comfortable yet leaving the kids in daycare with a stranger.

My seventh-grade year was the first year that our school started offering advanced classes, even though it was only math to start with. Ella and I were the only black people in that class. She didn't do so well, so about halfway through she was removed. I didn't think anything about being the only black person in the class.

I knew I was smart, and it felt good to learn at an advanced level since I felt like I was held back in my third-grade year. School was always a gender- and sexuality-free topic, which I appreciated; it was something that I could wallow in and not feel incompetent. But leaving the classroom meant I had to leave those distractions on the desk and be amongst my peers, who barely cared for school, bringing out the worst qualities in me and feeding my mental illnesses.

I had always been grateful that I was skinny and lacked curves like my other female friends who started maturing in elementary school. Ella and Tia were some of those girls. When my chest finally began to come in, I felt obligated to dress a bit more like a girl and give in to more aspects of femininity.

My sixth-grade relationships with boys validated my sexuality, but my gender identity was still on the fence until the changes that came along with puberty became more visible.

Turning twelve was my first chance to start playing basketball for my school on the modified team for seventh and eighth graders. Since I was a lowerclassman, I didn't get to start, but my ball handling skills landed me the position of the second-best point guard. Playing with the other girls showed me that I excelled at the sport. But I didn't see myself going that far with it after realizing I was only mediocre compared to the average black boy.

Regardless, I played because I had for basically my whole life and I didn't want my dad to make me feel like an idiot for wasting what he called "a God-given talent." All my dad's time and effort he spent believing in me made me a pretty good contender—for a girl, of course. Every time he came back to town from Charlotte, he would faithfully sit through my mediocre performances for Cheektowaga's team. I didn't like letting people down, and I was desperate to feel like a boy in any way, so I stayed with it.

He noticed my talents early on before moving to Charlotte and once I started spending summers with him, we played basketball in any free moments we had. My dad got more serious with me playing ball as I got closer to playing on my school teams and wanted me in the best condition possible. One summer he even put me in a basketball camp with a coach that once trained Steph Curry.

I wasn't impressed and refused to continue when I found out the camp had costed around $100 per week because I didn't want my dad to waste money on something I had no passion for.

My gender identity had been compromised as a member of the girls' basketball team, but it made me feel validated knowing that being good at sports linked my personality closer to that of a boy. Even though there were plenty of feminine girls on the team, I knew deep down I wasn't like them and that I didn't want to be.

It was hard to associate myself with their lifestyles outside of practice; they were all so cute I just wished I could've dated them instead. It also helped that the other point guard who was in the grade above was also a tomboy. I thought maybe being associated with that position would give people the allusion that we were one and the same: a masculine "female" who liked girls. It didn't, though, because we were two separate people and I hadn't yet tried to present as a male.

The complexities surrounding my gender identity and the natural pressures of competition started a shockwave of anxiety that I've dealt with for the past seven years. I had always been grouped with girls, but this time I felt exposed and humiliated having to play in games with not only my team but the other team of girls.

Playing in front of the crowd was the worst part because I was regularly in possession of the ball, so I knew all eyes were on me. I had seen small signs of anxiety growing up, but being the center of attention made things exponentially worse. For example, if I knew I was going to be late to an event, I would no longer want to go. I hate being the focus, and walking in late to anything or having a reason for everyone to pay attention to me feels like another form of public humiliation.

Both my mom and I noticed my anxiety surfacing more frequently in seventh grade. My coach was the first person to introduce the concept that being early is being on time, and she'd expect everyone at practice and ready to go fifteen minutes early. One day I woke up late for a Saturday practice and began feeling like it was the end of the world.

I immediately called Coach Colson and told her I was running late, and it seemed like no problem to her. As an emotional child, I was glad I didn't cry, because I literally didn't have the time. During the panic, I got frustrated trying to get into my mom's locked car and cut my finger somewhere along the way. When I showed up at practice, I was so frazzled that I didn't even notice all the blood on my clothes, hand, and water bottle that my coach pointed out. I had been so anxious that my mind didn't even process the pain.

As a result of this partly crippling mental illness, I was always caught up in my own thoughts. I knew I hated to be seen the way I was—as a girl, and not a boy—and it made me hate when people looked at me, even in passing. People judge based on first impressions, and it sickened me to know that most of the people I came across only saw me on the outside and had no idea that my mind and body didn't match.

Thankfully, my mom noticed my problems and sent me to counseling. I didn't fully understand what the session was at first, but I knew it could help ease my discomfort. The office was close to my house and very kid friendly. The first time I attended counseling, my mom was in the room since the therapist had to start by getting to know me and capturing an image of what my life was like at the time.

It went smoothly as far as I was concerned, and I thought every visit would be similar. I wasn't prepared for the way the sessions changed after the initial visit. The counselor wanted to delve deeper into my feelings during the second visit and asked my mom to sit outside the room. I can't remember what questions she asked me, but I will remember my answers forever.

"I don't want to be on...Earth anymore."

It was a nice way of saying "I wanna kill myself." At the time I didn't know what depression was or what suicide was, I just knew

I didn't like my life and that I felt so different from everyone else that I figured maybe I was in the wrong place. My internal battles seeped through during my first counseling experience.

My counselor tried to look further into my statement because she knew what I really wanted to say. But I wouldn't elaborate because I had no experience in expressing my feelings on such intimate topics. I also didn't want to worry her or anyone else that I might try to harm myself. At the same time, I was surprised at how open I felt with her. Something in her aura felt safe—safer than my own home.

My mom confronted me in the car after the appointment.

"You can't say stuff like that to people like her."

I didn't think the counselor would mention it, but I hadn't realized the weight of what I told her.

Not only wasn't I informed on mental illness, but I also didn't know places like psych wards existed and that I could potentially be sent to one for saying something like that. My mom did, which is why I missed my next appointment and every one after that. I wanted so badly to believe my mom just didn't like the lady who met with me, but it wasn't that. She was afraid of what I might say and the actions that would be taken if I continued to open up and reveal my depression.

The next week I went up to my mom and asked her, "Isn't it time to go to my appointment?" I didn't think she wouldn't take me back especially after the concerns from the counselor. I needed the help, though, so I had to ask.

"No, we're not going back there," she said, barely making eye contact with no explanation as to why.

Maybe she thought I didn't mean what I said, but I did. So I continued to suffer and never went back to that office again.

CHAPTER NINE

A Transition Toward Womanhood

Seventh grade continued to bring more insight on my personality, mental illnesses, and sexuality. One of my close friends from middle school, Randi, had a sleepover birthday party in a hotel with a bunch of other girls in our grade, including Tia. At that time, I wasn't as shy as I became later on, and I was still willing to swim in front of the other girls.

It caused me intense dysphoria to know they considered me one of them, especially when we were doing activities that were clearly separated by gender. I always wore one-piece bathing suits with little shorts to cover my bottom. I had seen other girls do it, and I always wondered if they did it for the same reasons I did.

The entire set up at the party was really nice. I was glad that I knew how to swim so I wouldn't have to feel left out in any other ways besides how I felt about the presentation of my identity. Since I was shy and didn't know everyone, I stayed close to Tia. Tia was closer to Randi than I was and knew all of her family that was there. When I first got there all the girls were spending a lot of time in the pool.

Tia and I were trying to do that cool thing where you open your eyes underwater. As I watched her hair float around in the water and her medium brown eyes reflect off the pool lights, I began to feel something towards her. That was the first time that I realized that I felt something more for her than I did for my other friends.

I came up above water acting like nothing had happened, but I knew that was a moment I would never forget.

After eating, we chilled by the pool and talked about the trending topic for preteen girls: boys. Tia, Randi, and another girl from our school named Caley were talking about sex. I didn't know much about sex except that it included genitals from both sexes. I also didn't have a boyfriend at all that entire year, so the thought of sex didn't even cross my mind. I didn't even want to imagine it.

If I was a cis male I probably would've thought about having sex with females but at that point in life, I believed it wasn't an option. It was hard for me to genuinely engage in conversation with my friends and Caley while they discussed those topics. How could I be so silent when I had dated so many guys in the past? Maybe I couldn't develop feelings for those boys because I was so young.

Or maybe the moment in the pool with Tia made me realize I wanted more than what those guys could offer. Deep down, I knew a woman could fulfill me and meet all of my emotional desires in ways that a man never could.

In April, I went on my first cruise to the Bahamas for my twelfth birthday. There were only adults that went including my auntie and nana who planned it out. My nana gets paranoid about violent acts like kidnappings, burglary, or any other type of crime. During our vacation, I was limited to activities I could do with the group in order to stay safe. Since I couldn't go anywhere by myself, I had to stay with an adult, which normally meant my nana since the other adults chose to go out and drink. It was weird; I knew we came for my birthday, but I felt like everyone else was having more fun than me.

My nana made me bring a dress onboard since we were having a formal dinner with the captain. I could see the awkward tension in my stance that came from dressing femininely. Having to be dressed like a female in front of so many strangers aboard the cruise heightened my anxiety and depression. After the dinner, I faced an emotional breakdown.

Nana didn't appreciate me having that intense moment of anxiety and told me to tighten up and get over it. Her words were so cold that I cuddled a blanket for comfort that night. My lack of understanding why I was upset made me feel like nana was right. Why was I always easily upset? I let myself feel sadness alone. I got anxiety from the thought of people knowing how I felt. Especially as a transman, growing up, I never wanted anyone to know the irregularity of my thought patterns as a cis female.

As the end of seventh grade approached, I started to become more conscious about how I dressed. After talking with my female friends at Randi's party and suffering through tears on the cruise, I thought it'd be best to advance my image as a girl. Toward the end of seventh grade, I began to dress more femininely, but since I had no real desire to wear skirts and dresses, my clothing choices ended up on the somewhat weird end of the spectrum.

My outfits often consisted of short shorts with leggings underneath and graphic tees. My friends were all surprised and shocked at my new attempts to suppress my persona as a tomboy. I should've known that the laughs from my friends and the discomfort within wouldn't last long. It was a role I wasn't good at pretending to play.

It was harder trying to obtain a female image with clothing more than presenting it with my sexuality. 2012 brought the famous teenage boy group Mindless Behavior. All my friends and cousins had big crushes on the members, but I didn't find them attractive the way all the other girls in my life did.

The only member of the group I liked was Princeton, and I'm pretty sure it's because he was my type in male form. The way I broadcasted my liking for him made me think I still had a chance at being heterosexual. But still, I wasn't as obsessed with him as I was with my other female celeb crushes like Zendaya and Paula Patton. Boys were first base, but girls were the home run.

Women have always been majorly present in my family, and when my dad got a new girlfriend, Amber, I was introduced to more. Unlike the others, she was here to stay, but I wanted to ask my dad, why this one? Amber had three daughters, two slightly older than me and one younger.

The girls were different from me; they lacked compliance, didn't care for school like I did, and stole from establishments and even people. Childhood environments have some of the biggest impacts on character development and personality. Based on their actions, I could tell that the girls were raised much differently than I was.

Their childhood wasn't centered in suburbia like mine was. As a result, we didn't get that close the first summer when we all lived in Charlotte together. My dad moved Amber and her daughters down into his two-bedroom townhouse at the same time that I came down for the summer.

I got to witness the girls adjust to a new surrounding that I had been somewhat part of for the last six years. Their new environment was inclusive of a foreign community, much warmer temperatures, and living with a man they didn't know.

My dad also had to undergo a change in habitat style once he was living with four females. No matter how nonchalant he acted, I knew he had a lot more to get used to with the girls than he let on. Living with someone is way harder than just seeing them in public spaces, especially someone who you don't understand.

That summer my dad commented on women in the most ignorant way possible. It had been about a year since I had first gotten my period, and I guess he'd noticed how seemingly unaffected my mood had been during that time. My dad doesn't believe in using anything as a crutch when you're down.

No headache meds, no limping or favoring a hurt spot, and he felt as if women used their period as an excuse to have mood swings. I wasn't sure where he got these ideals from, especially as a cisman, when he asked me, "How do you feel? You're on your menstrual right?"

I replied, "Yeah, I'm feeling good," because I did. But just because I felt fine doesn't mean that all women feel fine on their period or that I hadn't felt shitty during other months. I didn't conform to the stereotype of cravings and moodiness that month, but I did during other points throughout the year; my dad just caught me at a good time.

"See, don't listen to these women, they complain about being moody every time they get on their period. They don't really be moody, they just be using it as an excuse."

It was hard listening to stuff like that because I never knew what to say. I knew it wasn't true, of course, but at the young age of twelve I should always listen to my parents, right? That private incident between the two of us led me to believe that my dad and the girls would run into future conflict; I'm just glad I only had to experience the clash in personality differences for the summer. He simply doesn't understand anything that doesn't concern him, and frankly, he doesn't care to know.

I was glad the girls were down there with me, though. It meant I had to spend less time with him in his mostly empty car lot all day playing my PSP. Since I had started small efforts to dress more girly, I enlisted help from the girls to become more like them, further normalizing my gender identity.

When it was time to go back to school shopping, I got them involved. It felt like an uncomfortable transition into womanhood more than anything, which was harder because I was just starting to get there physically and I was still so far off from femininity in my mind. The only easy part about holding on to my cis identity was that everyone else in my life referred to me in all categories as female. I wanted a sense of stealth by hiding behind female clothes to avoid the negatives concerning how the world would judge me.

Kevin Thompson

I wanted to hide the female on the outside, but my passive nature figured if I could fly under the radar and look traditionally feminine then I would get less attention in public for being an outcast. But what I didn't know then was that your authentic self is the best version of yourself that you could ever be.

CHAPTER TEN

"I Think You're Gay"

When I went home for the summer, my mom decided that my back-to-school hairstyle should be micro braids. Micro braids are really small individual braids that can be braided with weave and styled in a variety of ways, depending on the kind of hair. I noticed how cute I looked in my feminine facade. The hair, tight clothes, and my growing chest started to distinguish me from masculinity. I tried coming into womanhood with open arms.

One of the first outfits that I wore to school that year was a white long sleeve thermal with red Hollister letters across the chest with some light blue skinny jeans and white sneakers. I was confident in my clothing choice for a girl, but still hadn't been fully in tune with every aspect associated with women. Even dressed up, I couldn't convince myself that I was like the other girls. My friends supported me moving forward, but they weren't so convinced either.

"That shirt is so cute, but you look awkward." Tia was never afraid to call me out.

"What do you mean?" Knowing me, I probably laughed.

"You don't look comfortable."

She was absolutely right, and the fact that I hadn't been visibly comfortable to outsiders worried me. Maybe I wasn't playing the part as well as I thought I was. It wouldn't just be my attire that would save me from outting myself as a societal outcast. It was

Kevin Thompson

my walk, the way I talked, even my posture. Everything but my clothes screamed boy.

As I struggled to perform my female act for the world, I decided to date boys again. The feeling of having a boyfriend and being called someone's girlfriend made me feel secure as a female. Jacob was my first and only boyfriend that year. Since we weren't able to talk much during school except for between classes, Jacob and I started writing a notebook and exchanged it during passing periods.

We wrote love letters to each other or just asked each other about general wellness. It was nice to have a companion who seemed to be my best friend with a little extra. I was still too young to think about sex, but also I didn't care to know. The little pecks and butterflies I got from entertaining guys was enough for me at the moment. I was mostly focused on myself and putting all of my energy towards achieving the female aesthetic. I thought I liked Jacob a lot because of his looks, and because the "relationship" had been going well, but I soon broke up with him...for a girl.

Something was happening in school that had previously been a foreign concept to all us kids: girls liking girls. There had been a plethora of girls coming out of the closet during basketball season that year. I was surprised at how well my other non-LGBTQ + friends responded. I appreciated the atmosphere and was also surprised that my elementary school crush, Kate, had been one of the girls to come out.

I remembered being upset as a child since I thought she would never like me because I was a girl, but that wasn't the case anymore. Still, I didn't stand a chance with Kate because I simply wasn't her type, female or male. Even though there were multiple girls coming out of the closet, each girl expressed their identities differently.

The visibility of someone's gender identity creates the stereotype that only people that look a certain way will be associated with a certain group. For example, men who wear tight jeans

58

and really short shorts are considered gay. Women, on the other hand, can avoid societal criticism while wearing male clothing. I figured that the girls who had still dressed full on feminine were more likely to label themselves as bi-curious.

A couple of my other friends, though, changed their clothing choices to mostly masuline which, in a way, outed their sexuality. Savanna was one of those girls. She dressed like a guy, so she got the "stud" label. Savanna and Kate quickly became an item before I had come out myself. Somehow, I couldn't see that Savanna had achieved what I wanted: successful masculinity as a female without ridicule, and the best part, Kate.

I looked up to Savanna and my other friend, Ariana, who played basketball with me because they dressed the way that I secretly wanted to. They reminded me of Jake, who passed completely for male without hormones, except that they seemed to be grounded in their gender as female. I wasn't totally convinced that Jake or I felt like women.

I was forced to sit on the sidelines for the first half of the season due to a concussion I obtained during soccer. I felt bad letting my teammates down for a sport I had only played once. The only reason that I decided to play soccer that year was because my gym teachers recognized my hidden talents in footwork that I developed playing ball and suggested that I join the team. It wasn't all bad on the sidelines, though. I got closer to some of the girls I had played with the year before during the time that I had been prohibited on the court.

Delanie was my first girlfriend. Her complexion was slightly lighter than mine and she was about 5'8. Laughter is the way to my heart, and that girl was hilarious. We sat next to each other in all our classes, in practice, and on those long bus rides to away games. My attention was fully centered on the center of our team.

I started getting closer to Delanie once she disclosed to me that she was also bi. I looked at her in a different light after she told me; I started noticing how smooth her caramel skin was and how cute her cheekbones were. It didn't take long before I told her that I liked girls too; she was the first person that I came out to concerning my sexuality.

"But don't you have a boyfriend?"

"Yeah, I'm bi, not gay."

I was mostly shy about admitting it at first since it was a part of me I had hidden for years. I became awkward about telling my boyfriend at the time. He probably wondered why I was having this realization in the midst of our relationship. Jacob was really chill about the whole thing, which I wasn't expecting. I also never expected him to be the first guy to come out to me. Jacob wrote me, "I'm pretty sure I'm bi, too," in our notebook of love letters.

I thought it was neat that Jacob was confident enough in his masculinity to admit that maybe he was attracted to guys. Some men who experience the common feeling of attraction toward the same sex tend to tense up and aggressievly deny the allegations. These men are sometimes the ones that just refuse to come out of the closet due to fear of ridicule.

I still didn't know if women or men were allowed to act on those kinds of feelings for the same sex. I also didn't know that so many girls and boys felt the same way I did. It made me feel more comfortable coming out at school since I knew I wouldn't be made fun of or singled-out. I started telling my friends that I was bi and got nothing but positive responses. Tia had even shared a moment like Delanie and I where she came out to me after I opened up to her.

Tia never dressed like a boy so I assumed that this would only be a phase for her. But I wasn't like Tia. I was like Savanna and Ariana, and when I found out Delanie liked me, I went through an immediate change in clothing and mentality. I felt the need to play the masculine role in our relationship for some reason, and

I hated the feminine compliments Delanie gave me when she called me beautiful. I knew that it didn't have to be that way; we could both be as feminine as we wanted and still be together, but I didn't want to be feminine anymore—I never did. I started wearing the only gender-neutral clothes that I owned.

Hoodies, jeans, sneakers and a ponytail were how I presented myself for the rest of 8th grade. I knew that people who had seen me in school every day witnessed my slight change in style, but I wasn't concerned with their opinions because of how great I felt in my own skin. I instantly felt more confident and happier with the alteration in my clothing.

That's how I knew it had been the right thing to do for myself. I had been more concerned about people's opinion before because I wanted to be "girly enough," and I was done pretending. Being comfortable about my sexuality made me unconsciously more comfortable with how I expressed my gender.

One Sunday night, I brought my mom in my room, sat her down and told her that I wanted to start dressing different. I laid out this outfit on my bed, black sweats and a white, long sleeve Michael Jordan shirt and said,

"This is what I want to start dressing like," I waited for her response in silent, not wanting to give away any more of my identity through our conversation.

She looked at me, then the clothes, then back at me and said, "Okay, do you have more stuff like that?"

It was supportive and a step in the right direction. I really wanted to say, "Let's throw out the whole damn closet and go shopping in the boys' section," but she wasn't there yet and I knew that. She wouldn't be for another couple years.

I dated Delanie for three weeks. We talked every day on the phone after school while I listened to 93.7 WBLK and watched out the window so I could hang up before my mom came in. In school, we would hug and kiss between classes. I still hadn't spent time with her out of school. I didn't want my mom to suspect anything. Even though I hadn't told her I liked girls, I kinda figured she might be able to catch on now that I dressed shamelessly like a tomboy.

Trying to be secretive, I came up with a plan to hang out with all three of my friends, including Delanie, at Ariana's house. It started out with all of us on my friend's bed, but my friends also had a plan to get me alone with Delanie. After about an hour, they left me and Delanie in the room. I was really nervous once I caught on to their tactics and realized that they were putting me in my first position to have sex. I ended up being too scared to do anything and stalling with phone games.

After a couple hours, we made our way out of the bedroom and into the living room with everyone else. Before I knew it, Delanie and I were alone again, this time with my arm around her watching 106 & Park. I felt a little embarrassed that I hadn't made any moves on my girlfriend since now I'd had multiple opportunities and more than enough time. My mom texted me and said she was on her way to come get me so I knew if anything was going to happen, now was the time to initiate it.

"Can I get a kiss before I leave?" I said to her while smiling with my eyes. She turned her whole body around, grabbed my face, and started making out with me. I counted that as my first real kiss, and I played love songs in my headphones the whole ride home.

Even though I had a girlfriend, I still felt a little something for Tia, and I could tell she was starting to have feelings for me too. At first, I thought Tia just felt closer to me since we were going through the same feelings of attraction for girls, but we started hanging out and spending the night over at each other's houses more than usual, so I figured something was going on.

I can always tell when a girl likes me, and Tia was making it obvious. From staring at me in science class, to making me miss my bus stop after school just to spend more time, to messaging me all day everyday on Kik, we got really close.

On March 8th, 2013, Rihanna kicked off the start of her Diamonds

World tour at the First Niagara Center in downtown Buffalo. My mom got tickets for me, my cousin Kayla, and my aunt. It was mine and Kayla's first concert, so our moms made a big deal about what we were gonna wear.

I wanted no part in choosing, so my mom chose for me. It was something purple with a skirt and leggings. I made sure to take pictures since I knew I could laugh with Tia about it later. I liked Tia because she could make me laugh at something that had the power to make me cry. Life is too short not to laugh.

She was very observant about my clothing and behavior during this period. Once we ceased our laughter about how ridiculous I looked at the concert, she said something that helped guide me to my current identity.

"I think you're gay."

I wasn't confused at her accusation, but I didn't feel gay or like a girl that liked girls. But it was true at the time, and it made more sense to be labeled gay than to be labled bisexual. Me being bi meant that I still liked boys, and with the absence of boys in my romantic life, I believed I could create a more masculine persona, so I went with it. I still felt as though something was missing. What I really wanted to be was a straight guy, but I did the best I could with what I had.

When it was time for her to leave that night, I walked her to my front door and before I said bye, she mentioned something.

"We been friends for years, but we never hugged..."

That was the new thing in school—when you liked someone, you hugged.

"Wow, I didn't even realize."

Before I could say anything else, Tia stepped in and wrapped her arms tight around my upper body. I reached for her waist and felt the warmth of her chest against mine. We hugged for a few seconds while I tried to take in her smell with my eyes closed. She let go and said goodbye with her head down as she walked out.

I reflected on our moment at my front door because of her touch making my body feel like it was releasing oxytocin. I liked hugging Tia more than I liked hugging my actual girlfriend, but I kept trying to find excuses that validated the moment like, "It was our first hug," or "I feel really comfortable around her since we've been friends for so long," but nothing was believable.

I ignored the signs between Tia and I for Delanie. It worked for a couple of weeks, but Tia and I would only be able to hide our love for so long.

CHAPTER ELEVEN

The Next Chapter

I started embracing my new label as a gay girl toward the end of my relationship with Delanie. Even though she ended things with me for another girl in our grade, we were still friends and even flirted a little. As soon as we were done, I told Delanie that I might like Tia. I was surprised at her dramatic reaction since she had been the one to leave me for someone else.

It was awkward because Tia and Delanie were also friends and actually talked to each other about how much they liked me in homeroom. Yeah, I thought it was weird, but it felt amazing having two friends like me at the same time and be open about it.

As always, I devoted my energy toward school. That year I had once again been put in Honors Math—aka Algebra 1—and Honors English class. There were three Honors classes offered that year, and the final one was Earth Science. I guess I never made the cut for that one, which turned out to be ironic since I'm now a Biology Major and have still never taken Earth Science. I could tell that things were going to get harder, but the rigor felt normal until high school.

That year, when the City Honors and Olmstead entry exams occurred, my mom dragged me in. She had no intention of me going to either school; she just wanted to see if I could pass the test. It was a cold Saturday morning and I was sick with a cold.

They made us go in the auditorium and fill out a sheet about which school we would like to be admitted to if we got adequate exam scores. Usually, City Honors takes the best students and Olmstead takes the second best. I had no preference for either school so I just put both. After a small introduction from faculty at both schools, all the students were led into a series of classrooms based on alphabetical order. The test was long like the SAT and had breaks in between parts.

The test wasn't easy, but it also wasn't hard. I wasn't sure how well I did in the multiple choice section, but I knew I killed it on the writing section. In 8th grade English Honors we worked on writing from a variety of perspectives. I decided to put my skills to use that I learned in class for the test's writing portion.

The task was to write an essay on the life of a one-hundred-year-old penny. I switched up the perspective and wrote about the penny in first person as if I were the penny. I felt successful and witty about my stylistic choices since I knew many other students wouldn't take the same approach. It was one of my best creative writing moments.

Everyone who knew I had taken the entrance exam asked how it was since most people wouldn't be able to pass. I said it was tricky because I could tell that they wanted to trip students up on some of the questions; only the sharpest would survive.

Some of my teachers in eighth grade knew I went in for the test and begged for updates on my exam scores. My social studies teacher at the time was the most supportive and believed I could pass the test. I realized that if I got in, they would expected me to go and to not pass up the opportunity. I also realized I wasn't ready to leave my friends and be forced to start high school alone.

When I started dating Delanie, I also started hanging around some of her friends in school, including Aaliyah and Sydney. Sydney enjoyed calling me "son" for whatever reason. I always laughed and enjoyed when she called me that since it put me in a male light. I liked the association a little too much to be cis. When my social studies teacher watched me go through changes concerning my gender, she also witnessed my behavior change.

I wasn't bad, but I cared less and since I was smart, I helped my new friend group cheat in her class. My teacher started commenting on my new persona, but I didn't mind. Maybe I had been too much of a goody-two-shoes before. I had a lot to be proud of, and I knew there were only certain lines that I would cross when it came to breaking the rules.

I had never gotten in trouble at school or at home, but that changed once my mom found out about my gender identity. I came out of the closet involuntarily when my mom went through my cellphone in March of 2013. My mom found out about Delanie and I after reading the messages between us. Of course my mom was mad at me for being in a relationship at such a young age, but she wasn't mad that I liked girls, which I was grateful for.

I thought it would've been clear to her and everyone else that I was gay since I went through such a dramatic shift in clothing, but I guess they were in denial. My dad barely reacted to the situation and assumed, as did my mom, that I was going through a phase. I knew they were wrong since I remembered liking girls as far back as preschool.

They probably thought that I was more likely to go through a stage of liking girls since I was a girl. I felt invalidated by their accusations and began to get frustrated that I couldn't seem to convince them that this was who I was.

My stepdad was there the day my mom found the messages, but he had nothing to say. I didn't know what he would say if he did, but I'm glad he didn't. He and I both knew that it was better for him to keep his two cents to himself since my mom would always take my side, no matter what. She was definitely not the kind of parent that would neglect their own child for a significant other. Kids should always take priority.

My mom didn't really want me to tell the rest of my family since "it wasn't their business," but it made me feel like being gay was something to hide. It felt like something I should be ashamed of, but why?

I don't recall how my nana found out, but the conversation with her is one of the only ones I remember. The rest of my family was at a loss for words, and there was really nothing to say anyway.

"How are you gonna have sex?" she asked, even though I was only 13.

I didn't have a response for her because I was still a virgin. I was surprised that she brought up sex at all since I was so young. Did she figure that I had been sexually active and that I had made my decision based off of merely sexual acts? The thing she didn't know was that it wasn't about sex. It was never about just sex for me. I had felt this way about girls even before I knew what sex was. If you're attracted to someone, trust me, you will find a way to make sex work for the both of you—with some practice, of course. Sex is sex no matter the gender.

Track was the new hype after basketball season was over. Delanie was also on our modified track team, but I wasn't talking to her on the phone after school anymore. I was doing pushups and listening to Chris Brown's Fortune album instead.

One of the girls who was part of my friend group with Randi was Alyssa, and I spent most of my time at practice with her. Alyssa was quiet, but she was so funny once she started talking. She was the first to notice a slight change in my body after I started working out at home. I thought she only noticed because we were friends, but I'd later learn that our relationship wasn't totally platonic.

I started getting more attention from girls that year; it was the first time that I was single and out of the closet. It seemed that I found out about other girls that liked me on a frequent basis. Life was going well, and on top of my social success, I had just received my acceptance letter to City Honors. It was essentially the equivalent of getting accepted to an ivy league high school.

I didn't know how great the school was until I got in. Everyone kept congratulating me on my acceptance, but I didn't get why they had been so proud. Upon my acceptance, I was invited to a shadowing day at my future school. The atmosphere there was very different than my previous school. It was calm, quiet, and mostly white. I could tell that the work was difficult and that the students were academically advanced; I liked the sense of prestige in the air.

That day I decided that City Honors would be the next step in my life. But not going there was never really an option; my mom insisted that I go and not give up the opportunity, even though we didn't live in the district.

That meant that I would have to start over and leave my friends at Cheektowaga. I knew I was going to miss Tia more than anyone. She was happy for me, but she was also sad to see me leave the school we grew up in. It would suck not being able to see her on a daily basis since it was clear that we liked each other.

Tia had a boyfriend, Sean, at that time, but he didn't care if she liked me. I had also dated Sean during my sixth grade streak with boys, but now his annoying personality was no longer cute. He saw her feelings toward other females as invalid. I would get so frustrated watching them together in school when Tia and I had our own thing going on; those hugs between us between classes always lasted a bit too long. I also hated the feeling of inadequacy.

Sean perceived me as a girl and therefore our feelings were something artificial that wouldn't last. Maybe she did like me, but her status as bi subjected her to the stigma that bi girls are only curious, not genuinely attracted to other girls. He was confident, but I was more confident. I knew Tia for years, and she didn't care about Sean.

For our eighth-grade trip to Washington, D.C., students were able to pick who they would be sharing a hotel room with. I knew that if me and Tia had any alone time in that room then something would go down. There was four of us: me, Randi, Brittney and Tia. I planned to share a bed with Randi since me and Tia were keeping our "thing" on the downlow. I didn't want anyone to catch on to our flirtatious interactions. Even sitting next to her on the bus ride there felt a bit revealing.

That night once we got settled in, the girls and I hung out in the room, scrolling different apps and making each other laugh. Randi was out first, and Brittany stayed up a bit with me and Tia. I didn't stay up on purpose to be alone with Tia, but the next thing I knew, Brittany was sleeping on the same bed next to Randi.

There was no waking her up, so I knew that Tia and I would be sleeping with each other for the night. It started out with the two of us going through Tumblr and listening to music, but then Tia went quiet and just stared at me. I thought it was weird because she did it for so long, but then I figured out what she was staring for. She wanted to kiss me.

"Oh...you wanna kiss?"

She nodded yes while still maintaining eye contact.

"I don't think we should. You're dating Sean, I don't want you to cheat on him."

While she laid next to me and tried to explain how irrelevant he was, I thought about actually kissing her. I didn't care about if she had a boyfriend or not, I was scared to take what we had to the next level since we had been friends for almost 5 years.

I didn't want anything to change between the two of us if we ended up not working out. But I liked her a lot and after about an hour of talking, I decided to just go for it.

"Fuck it." I said, and rolled over to kiss her.

When Tia and I had our first kiss, I felt something special. I had never felt that way with Delanie—or with anyone, for that matter. We rolled over on top of each other for what seemed like a minute until she stopped us and said,

"We're getting really hot really fast. I want to stop."

"Why?" I didn't know what I was gonna do next, but I didn't want to stop.

"I can get really carried away really fast."

I didn't know exactly what she meant by that, but I knew it involved sexual things that I couldn't even imagine. Tia had already been sexually experimenting with other people, both boys and girls. She had more knowledge in the bedroom, and I wanted to learn, but that would have to wait.

I fell asleep with a stuffy nose in her arms in the early hours of the morning. We only got a couple hours of sleep before our second day in Washington D.C., but I wouldn't have changed it for the world. We did a lot of sight-seeing that day. The sun was beaming down on us, and as the heat rose it felt like our sexual tension rose along with it.

We ended the day on a fancy dinner cruise that everyone dressed up for. I wore a white polo shirt and khakis with my hair down. I thought having my hair down instead of in my normal ponytail would make me fancier for the occasion. Tia wore a dress and I thought she looked better than usual, but it was probably just my feelings that looked better on her. Her personality was starting to light up my heart.

Our second and last night in Washington was spent in a bed with Brittney. All three of us had been on our phones in one bed while Randi slept in the other. When Brittney finally fell asleep next to us, me and Tia were right back to making out. I laid on top of her and we kissed in the quiet of the night, right next to our sleeping friend.

We both agreed that we felt like we were in a dream. It felt surreal kissing her after all of our small and intimate moments. I wanted another night with her, but I knew we'd be going home in the morning, so I held her as tight as I could until the sun rose.

CHAPTER TWELVE

Goodbyes

The bus back to Buffalo stopped at Starbucks before getting on the road. I went in with Brittney and Randi went to sit on the bus with Tia. Brittney had started to bring up what was going on with me and Tia.

"You can tell?" I tried to play it off at first, but I also didn't want to lie to our friends.

"Yeah, it's pretty obvious. What did you guys do when we went to sleep?" Brittney asked, but we both knew that she knew what happened.

"We made out," I said proudly, still amazed at the fact that I could even land girls.

When we got home, everything seemed to go back to normal at school. Tia and I hugging in the hallway and Sean still getting on my nerves. I spent my hours after school talking to Tia on my cellphone and listening to music. I started to get into Alternative Rock during the last few months of middle school after my English teacher played some Imagine Dragons and Linkin Park during our writing periods.

I got my first pair of beats and wore them all the time, sometimes falling asleep in them. Tia would always stay up late with me and talk while I discovered new bands and songs. We got closer and talked about personal topics like depression and sex. I knew that the next time she stayed over that we would take it there.

The next time after Washington that Tia and I slept in the same vicinity was for my siblings' second birthday. Unfortunately, there were new rules for me since the last time she had spent the night. Now that my mom was aware I liked girls, she had to establish boundaries.

Since Tia and I had plenty of sleepovers in the past, she probably wouldn't be mistaken for a possible romantic partner. Our friendship title had landed us the freedom to be alone together, but now there was a catch. She could sleep over, but I couldn't sleep with her.

"You can stay in your room and she can stay in the basement."

My mom was slightly confused at what to do with me now that she knew my sexual orientation. I couldn't have sleepovers with girls, but I couldn't have sleepovers with boys either. I didn't fight with her because I knew I could still have some privacy with Tia in the basement after the party.

Once the house went to sleep, me and Tia played music in the basement and practiced grinding on each other. Things got spicy when she took control of me, put me in a chair, and then pushed me against the wall. I was shocked at how well she moved her body, and I knew she was about to teach me what sex was.

The lights went off, and our clothes came off while the music stayed on. Since I was ashamed of my own body, I left on my shorts and a sports bra. I didn't want her to touch me and think of me as a girl, especially during sex, so I kept the focus on her. It was dark, and I couldn't see what I was doing as I reached down below her waist.

She moved my hands to the right places and whispered some directions in my ear; she knew exactly what she wanted and how to get there. I told her I loved her for the first time, and I meant it. She replied with an, "I love you too," that I could see in her medium brown eyes. I couldn't believe that she was still with Sean after all that.

My feelings for her had been building for months, and they were finally starting to come out after our first time together. The fact that we were friends made me more comfortable and sure that we would last if we decided to be together. I just needed Sean out the picture.

It was mid-June, and as the end of the year approached, I began to say my goodbyes. Graduation was coming and I wouldn't be coming back to Central when school picked back up in September. When I was saying bye to Ashlyn, she told me that she had a crush on me since I had been out as gay.

"Why are you telling me this now?"

I almost said, "Why didn't you tell me sooner?" but I was glad she didn't. I wouldn't have known what to do with that information since I hadn't felt the same way. She spared us plenty of awkward moments and we had the opportunity to go out as just friends.

I questioned why I had so many girls reveal their feelings for me after coming out. They were probably just impressed and attracted to the fact I was unapologetically me.

I knew that with graduation coming up, I was going to have to dress up, but not in the way I got away with in D.C.. This time my family was going to be there, and we would be taking lasting pictures to recollect the day.

"You have to wear a dress. These are the pictures that are going to last forever." That was my dad's way of saying, "You're going to thank me later when you look back at these pictures once you are out of your phase." But he was wrong this time. Now all I think about looking back at my graduation pictures from eighth grade is my family trying to justify me wearing clothes that I didn't feel comfortable in.

I was miserable, scrounging through various stores in the mall with Kayla and my aunt. Every dress was just so girly; there was no avoiding a feminine presence for the big day. I gave up trying to look for anything that would coincide with what I really wanted to wear, and as my family dragged me around the rest of the mall trying to pick out something that would look good on me, I devised a plan to bring an extra set of clothes to school to change into.

It wouldn't be easy, though, since everyone would be there to witness me in an outfit that wasn't approved by my mom. She picked out this vintage reddish, yellow, and orange dress with a jean jacket. I remember looking at it and saying to myself, "That's a cute outfit, just not for me." I didn't want to bear the pain of shopping, so I just said yes to whatever my mom choose.

I looked good, and I would've looked even better if I was actually meant to be a girl. My awkward ways of not knowing how to act in that dress just made me look and feel like shit. One of my sixth-grade exes, Darren, didn't agree.

"Wow, you look beautiful."

Cringing inside, I tried to smile and thank him for the kind words, but I wished he hadn't said anything at all. His compliment reminded me of how people were perceiving me that day. I hate that people's last image of me at that school was in a dress. Despite the frustration, I tried to appreciate the compliments and I promised myself that I would never put on a dress again.

I got through graduation and went back to trying to dress neutrally. Now that it was summertime, I couldn't get away with my usual jeans and hoodie outfits. I fished through my auntie's closet at times since she had a bit of a neutral style of dressing. New clothing wasn't the only thing I was trying that summer.

Tia broke up with Sean once school was out. Since no one my age had cars or jobs, my friends spent a lot of time outside and at the park. One day in June I met up with Brittney and Tia to chill before I left for Charlotte that summer. Originally, it was supposed to only be the three of us, but more of our friends from school like Delanie and Ariana showed up.

I knew that both Ariana and Delanie were heavy smokers even

though they were only thirteen; they had both started in seventh grade. I had never been afraid to smoke and knew I would if I had the opportunity, I just didn't know anything about the process of getting it, rolling it, or smoking it.

I didn't plan to smoke that day. All of us left the park to go get my friend's charger from her house. Since we were close to the plug, Ariana and Delanie decided to go pick up a nick, a $5 bag of weed. I wanted to go with them so that I could smoke and have time to be high before going home.

We walked up to a street corner on the border of the city and the suburbs. It was an odd but quick interaction, and the three of us left to go back to the park. We smoked under a bridge, and, unlike the rest of society, I had no problem inhaling and suffered through minimal coughing. When the blunt was out, I complained to them about not feeling anything. I had never been around anyone who had just smoked except for Ariana, and I could tell both of them were high.

"Don't worry, you'll feel it as soon as you stand up." Ariana laughed, but I didn't believe her since I hadn't felt anything yet.

We started walking back to the Rec. center that had a hockey rink and tables inside. As soon as we came out from under the bridge and started our trek, the whole world began to move from side to side. I remember feeling drunk, not knowing which way to walk, and not being able to stand. Delanie picked me up with dirt stains on my pants and kissed me. Wait, I thought we were only friends?

I was too high to process the moment with Delanie and followed my two friends inside the Rec Tia and Brittney were sitting at the tables, not really amused at the state I was in, especially Tia.

"You were supposed to be spending the day with me and Brittney, but now you're high as shit."

I could tell Tia was angry with me, but my high-spirited mind couldn't be sad or feel sympathy for her in the situation. I was barely functioning, jumping on tables and lying face down on benches with my limbs hanging off. I'm just glad I was with friends, because I desperately needed to be watched.

Eventually, Tia got fed up with me and my idiotic ways and left while flipping me off and not saying a word. I yelled, "Noo, come back!" but my tone was dramatic, so all my friends laughed while I sat on the bench watching the love of my life walk out the door. I knew I messed up.

My aunt picked me up and I sprawled out on the backseat for the entire car ride, claiming I was tired. She asked me to go into my house and bring out some of her clothes that I had worn the week before. I was so high that I brought the clothes to my mom.

"Why you giving those to me?" Shit, I needed to perk up and act sober; she couldn't catch me already, it was only my first time. I brought the clothes out, came back in the house, and passed out, waking up to no new messages from Tia.

That was my second summer with the girls in Charlotte. I figured if my stepsisters were bad enough to steal, they would be bad enough to smoke, and I was right. My family back in Buffalo thought that the girls were the reason that I started smoking. Truthfully, they weren't the best influences, but I had already been exposed to marijuana.

I spent my graduation money on weed for me and the two oldest girls after we found a dealer at an apartment complex that we visited regularly across the street. You'd be surprised at how easy it is to find weed these days.

My oldest stepsister met a guy in the apartment complex that we used to hang out at since there were more kids our age there than where we lived. That summer I wasn't trying to be girly. I didn't tell my sisters that I liked girls, but I'm pretty sure they could tell from the way I had begun to dress.

They eventually found out the truth once we all talked about romantic interests because I mentioned Tia. I guess it didn't really click for my sisters that me liking girls wasn't a phase because they tried hooking me up with guys anyway.

Most days, my dad and stepmom would go to work and one of the sisters would go to camp or summer school, but the oldest and I would have the house to ourselves. She frequently invited her new boyfriend over, so I always made my way to the upstairs shower and conducted concerts to combat any unwanted sounds. But one day, she told me her boyfriend was bringing a friend for me.

"Not for me, I'm not going to like him."

"You haven't even seen him yet."

I didn't have to.

When they arrived I didn't run to the shower. I didn't want a rando in my house by himself so I thought maybe he'd see how gay I was and we could chill as friends while my sister and his friend did their thing. But teenage boys are made horny and with little consideration toward females, so there was no "chilling" with this guy.

The guy shoved me to the back room while my sister and her boyfriend were in the living room. To this day, I never understood why my sister didn't just take the room like she always had. Maybe this was a setup...for me.

"I told you I don't like guys, I really don't."

He shut the door and threw me on the bed.

Most people are unaware that sexual abuse can mean more than just being raped. There's a lot of other things that someone can do that are still nonconsensual and violating even if it's not the kind of sexual assault you hear about in the media.

When the boy started tugging at my basketball shorts, I fought him and he threw me around until I was on my stomach. I ended up on the edge of the bed, and he rubbed his hands over me while dry humping me from behind.

"Why you gotta be gay? You can be bi," he whispered in my ear while still holding his weight on top of me.

After about five minutes of me clearly not enjoying the encounter, he stopped, got off, and left. He probably figured, "Man this girl is actually gay."

I never even caught his name. I couldn't imagine ever liking men again.

END BOOK 1

Self-Made Man: Book 2

In the continuation of Self-Made Man, Kevin starts school at City Honors. With depression on his back, Kevin discovers he is transgender. His relationship fails and his use of drugs increases. After the death of someone in Kevin's household, he prepares for college and the start of medically transitioning.

Made in the USA
Middletown, DE
27 September 2019